Knock! Knock! Who's There?

ARCTURUS

ARCTURUS

This edition published in 2017 by Arcturus Publishing Limited
26/27 Bickels Yard, 151–153 Bermondsey Street,
London SE1 3HA

ISBN: 978-1-78428-478-7
CH005154NT
Supplier 29, Date 0517, Print run 5780

Written by Lisa Regan
Illustrated by Shutterstock
Designed by Trudi Webb
Edited by Tracey Kelly

Printed in China

CONTENTS

KNOCK, KNOCK.
WHO'S THERE?
MEGAN.
MEGAN WHO?
MEGAN A MESS OUT HERE, HELP ME CLEAN UP!

KNOCK, KNOCK.
WHO'S THERE?
LUKE.
LUKE WHO?
LUKE THROUGH THE KEYHOLE!

KNOCK, KNOCK.
WHO'S THERE?
ALI.
ALI WHO?
ALI WANNA DO IS HAVE SOME FUN!

KNOCK, KNOCK.
WHO'S THERE?
HUGH.
HUGH WHO?
HUGH DO YOU THINK YOU ARE?

KNOCK, KNOCK.
WHO'S THERE?
DIDDY.
DIDDY WHO?
DIDDY HURT HIMSELF PLAYING FOOTBALL?

KNOCK, KNOCK.
WHO'S THERE?
WYNN.
WYNN WHO?
WYNN THE DELIVERY MAN COMES, SIGN THE FORM.

KNOCK, KNOCK.
WHO'S THERE?
LIZ.
LIZ WHO?
LIZ GO OUT TONIGHT!

KNOCK, KNOCK.
WHO'S THERE?
ABBY.
ABBY WHO?
ABBY-CADABRA,
THAT'S MAGIC!

KNOCK, KNOCK.
WHO'S THERE?
METEOR.
METEOR WHO?
METEOR ON THE
CORNER IN FIVE
MINUTES!

KNOCK, KNOCK.
WHO'S THERE?
MUSTAFA.
MUSTAFA WHO?
MUSTAFA SLEEPOVER SOON, I HAVEN'T SEEN YOU FOR AGES!

KNOCK, KNOCK.
WHO'S THERE?
SIRIOUS.
SIRIOUS WHO?
SIRIOUSLY, LET ME IN, IT'S FREEZING OUT HERE!

KNOCK, KNOCK.
WHO'S THERE?
CONSTANCE.
CONSTANCE WHO?
CONSTANCE SHOUTING NEXT DOOR IS GETTING ON MY NERVES!

KNOCK, KNOCK.
WHO'S THERE?
PAM.
PAM WHO?
PAMDEMONIUM IN THE STREET, COME AND LOOK!

KNOCK, KNOCK.
WHO'S THERE?
HARDY.
HARDY WHO?
HARDY ANYONE AROUND THIS WEEKEND!

KNOCK, KNOCK.
WHO'S THERE?
WALTER.
WALTER WHO?
WALTER PATHETIC LITTLE DOOR KNOCKER THIS IS!

KNOCK, KNOCK.
WHO'S THERE?
JEROME.
JEROME WHO?
JEROME AT LONG LAST, WHERE HAVE YOU BEEN?

KNOCK, KNOCK.
WHO'S THERE?
WAITER.
WAITER WHO?
WAITER MINUTE, MY PHONE IS RINGING!

KNOCK, KNOCK.
WHO'S THERE?
CANDACE.
CANDACE WHO?
CANDACE BE TRUE—YOU PASSED YOUR EXAMS?

KNOCK, KNOCK.
WHO'S THERE?
SHEILA.
SHEILA WHO?
SHEILA-VOID YOU, I'M AFRAID SHE DOESN'T LIKE ANYONE.

KNOCK, KNOCK.
WHO'S THERE?
IMOGEN.
IMOGEN WHO?
IMOGEN IF WE DIDN'T HAVE TO GO TO SCHOOL NEXT WEEK!

KNOCK, KNOCK.
WHO'S THERE?
IKE.
IKE WHO?
IKE COULD HAVE WALKED RIGHT IN, THE DOOR IS UNLOCKED!

KNOCK, KNOCK.
WHO'S THERE?
CHER.
CHER WHO?
CHER YOUR TREATS,
OR I'LL TELL
EVERYONE YOU'RE A
MEANIE.

KNOCK, KNOCK.
WHO'S THERE?
JUPITER.
JUPITER WHO?
JUPITER HURRY, I
REALLY NEED THE
BATHROOM!

KNOCK, KNOCK.
WHO'S THERE?
HOWARD.
HOWARD WHO?
HOWARD YOU LIKE IT IF I
TOOK YOU TO THE MOVIES?

KNOCK, KNOCK.
WHO'S THERE?
FARMER.
FARMER WHO?
FARMER DISTANCE YOU LOOK JUST LIKE YOUR DAD!

KNOCK, KNOCK.
WHO'S THERE?
WILLY.
WILLY WHO?
WILLY EVER GET AROUND TO TIDYING HIS ROOM?

KNOCK, KNOCK.
WHO'S THERE?
ESAU.
ESAU WHO?
ESAU AN OLD FRIEND AND HAS GONE AROUND FOR LUNCH.

41

KNOCK, KNOCK.
WHO'S THERE?
ALF.
ALF WHO?
ALF FEED YOUR CAT WHILE YOU'RE AWAY, IF YOU LIKE.

KNOCK, KNOCK.
WHO'S THERE?
SUE.
SUE WHO?
SUE-PER HERO AT YOUR SERVICE!

KNOCK, KNOCK.
WHO'S THERE?
ALISON.
ALISON WHO?
ALISON AT THE DOOR TO HEAR WHEN YOU WERE COMING.

45

KNOCK, KNOCK.
WHO'S THERE?
WALLACE.
WALLACE WHO?
WALLACE IS A COINCIDENCE, FANCY SEEING YOU!

KNOCK, KNOCK.
WHO'S THERE?
JESTER.
JESTER WHO?
JESTER MINUTE, MY PHONE'S RINGING.

KNOCK, KNOCK.
WHO'S THERE?
MCKEE.
MCKEE WHO?
MCKEE WON'T TURN IN THE LOCK!

50

KNOCK, KNOCK.
WHO'S THERE?
PIET.
PIET WHO?
PIET OF ADVICE FOR
YOU—DON'T EAT
YELLOW SNOW!

KNOCK, KNOCK.
WHO'S THERE?
ANITA.
ANITA WHO?
ANITA ESSAY WOULD
HAVE BEEN GIVEN A
BETTER GRADE.

KNOCK, KNOCK.
WHO'S THERE?
TOBY.
TOBY WHO?
TOBY OR NOT TOBY, THAT
IS THE QUESTION!

KNOCK, KNOCK.
WHO'S THERE?
LEONA.
LEONA WHO?
LEONA OF THAT CAR HAS PARKED IN YOUR DRIVEWAY!

KNOCK, KNOCK.
WHO'S THERE?
SID.
SID WHO?
SID DOWN, I HAVE SOME SHOCKING NEWS.

KNOCK, KNOCK.
WHO'S THERE?
DEXTER.
DEXTER WHO?
DEXTER HALLS WITH BOUGHS OF HOLLY!

53

KNOCK, KNOCK.
WHO'S THERE?
ESTHER.
ESTHER WHO?
ESTHER ANYTHING YOU WANT ME TO GET FOR YOU IN TOWN?

KNOCK, KNOCK.
WHO'S THERE?
USHER.
USHER WHO?
USHER BYE BABY, ON THE TREETOP...

KNOCK, KNOCK.
WHO'S THERE?
COLIN.
COLIN WHO?
COLIN A DOCTOR— I'M SICK!

KNOCK, KNOCK.
WHO'S THERE?
AL.
AL WHO?
AL LET YOU INTO A SECRET...

KNOCK, KNOCK.
WHO'S THERE?
SEYMOUR.
SEYMOUR WHO?
SEYMOUR FROM YOUR UPSTAIRS WINDOW!

KNOCK, KNOCK.
WHO'S THERE?
ALICE.
ALICE WHO?
ALICE-N AT THE DOOR TO SEE IF YOU'RE HOME!

61

KNOCK, KNOCK.
WHO'S THERE?
JOANNA.
JOANNA WHO?
JOANNA GO FOR A WALK?

KNOCK, KNOCK.
WHO'S THERE?
MICKEY.
MICKEY WHO?
MICKEY IS STUCK IN THE LOCK!

KNOCK, KNOCK.
WHO'S THERE?
PHYLLIS.
PHYLLIS WHO?
PHYLLIS BUCKET, PLEASE, I'M WASHING THE CAR!

KNOCK, KNOCK.
WHO'S THERE?
MISTY.
MISTY WHO?
MISTY DOORBELL AND KNOCKED INSTEAD!

KNOCK, KNOCK.
WHO'S THERE?
ALEX.
ALEX WHO?
ALEX MY ICE CREAM TO KEEP IT FROM MELTING DOWN MY ARM.

KNOCK, KNOCK.
WHO'S THERE?
CAMERON
CAMERON WHO?
CAMEROND 8 O'CLOCK AND WE'LL WALK TOGETHER.

83

KNOCK, KNOCK.
WHO'S THERE?
TANK.
TANK WHO?
TANK WHO VERY MUCH!

KNOCK, KNOCK.
WHO'S THERE?
BEAVER E.
BEAVER E. WHO?
BEAVER E. QUIET SO YOU DON'T WAKE THE BABY!

KNOCK, KNOCK.
WHO'S THERE?
PATTY.
PATTY WHO?
PATTY YOUR DOORBELL DOESN'T WORK, I'VE BEEN STANDING HERE FOR AGES.

KNOCK, KNOCK.
WHO'S THERE?
EVAN.
EVAN WHO?
EVAN THOUGH IT'S RAINING, YOU WON'T LET ME IN?

KNOCK, KNOCK.
WHO'S THERE?
PAUL.
PAUL WHO?
PAUL OLD FELLA HAS HURT HIS KNEE.

KNOCK, KNOCK.
WHO'S THERE?
NAT.
NAT WHO?
NAT A PROBLEM THAT WE'RE HERE, IS IT?

KNOCK, KNOCK.
WHO'S THERE?
A WAYNE.
A WAYNE WHO?
A WAYNE IN A MANGER!

KNOCK, KNOCK.
WHO'S THERE?
DAN.
DAN WHO?
DAN DAN DA! IT'S ME!
SURPRISE!

KNOCK, KNOCK.
WHO'S THERE?
SPELL.
SPELL WHO?
W-H-O. EASY!

KNOCK, KNOCK.
WHO'S THERE?
FELINE.
FELINE WHO?
FELINE GOOD TODAY!

KNOCK, KNOCK.
WHO'S THERE?
CARRIE.
CARRIE WHO?
CARRIE THESE BAGS, THERE ARE MORE IN THE CAR.

KNOCK, KNOCK.
WHO'S THERE?
MANNY.
MANNY WHO?
MANNY PEOPLE HAVE LIVED IN THIS HOUSE BUT YOU'RE THE NICEST!

96

KNOCK, KNOCK.
WHO'S THERE?
WANDA.
WANDA WHO?
WANDA IF THERE'S ANYTHING GOOD ON THE TV TONIGHT?

KNOCK, KNOCK.
WHO'S THERE?
VASSAR.
VASSAR WHO?
VASSAR MATTER, ARE YOU CRYING?

KNOCK, KNOCK.
WHO'S THERE?
KENT.
KENT WHO?
KENT YOU DO YOUR HOMEWORK?

KNOCK, KNOCK.
WHO'S THERE?
GABE.
GABE WHO?
GABE YOU A CALL BUT IT WENT STRAIGHT TO VOICEMAIL.

KNOCK, KNOCK.
WHO'S THERE?
LEIF.
LEIF WHO?
LEIF ME ALONE, I'M IN A BAD MOOD!

KNOCK, KNOCK.
WHO'S THERE?
CATH.
CATH WHO?
CATH ON DELIVERY, PLEATHE?

KNOCK, KNOCK.
WHO'S THERE?
JOE.
JOE WHO?
JOE KNOW THE WAY TO THE PARK?

KNOCK, KNOCK.
WHO'S THERE?
BECCA.
BECCA WHO?
BECCA THE BUS IS WHERE THE ROWDY KIDS SIT!

KNOCK, KNOCK.
WHO'S THERE?
TRUDI.
TRUDI WHO?
TRUDI SCRUMPTIOUS!

109

113

KNOCK, KNOCK.
WHO'S THERE?
HARDY.
HARDY WHO?
HARDY RECOGNIZED YOU WITH YOUR NEW HAIRCUT!

KNOCK, KNOCK.
WHO'S THERE?
OMAR.
OMAR WHO?
OMAR GOODNESS, I'M AT THE WRONG ADDRESS!

KNOCK, KNOCK.
WHO'S THERE?
COOK.
COOK WHO?
THAT'S THE FIRST CUCKOO I'VE HEARD THIS YEAR!

KNOCK, KNOCK.
WHO'S THERE?
WATER.
WATER WHO?
WATER YOU WAITING FOR? LET'S GO!

KNOCK, KNOCK.
WHO'S THERE?
BETH.
BETH WHO?
BETH TIME FOR YOU, YOU'RE FILTHY!

KNOCK, KNOCK.
WHO'S THERE?
GHANA.
GHANA WHO?
GHANA HAVE A SANDWICH, DO YOU WANT ONE?

KNOCK, KNOCK.
WHO'S THERE?
KENNY.
KENNY WHO?
KENNY FIND OUT WHY THE POLICE CALLED NEXT DOOR?

KNOCK, KNOCK.
WHO'S THERE?
EWAN.
EWAN WHO?
EWAN ME ARE BEST FRIENDS!

KNOCK, KNOCK.
WHO'S THERE?
MAX.
MAX WHO?
MAX NO DIFFERENCE, JUST LET ME IN!

129

KNOCK, KNOCK.
WHO'S THERE?
IVA.
IVA WHO?
IVA BANANA, IT'S
REALLY DELICIOUS!

KNOCK, KNOCK.
WHO'S THERE?
BENNY.
BENNY WHO?
BENNY THING
GOOD ON TV,
TONIGHT?

KNOCK, KNOCK.
WHO'S THERE?
DORIS.
DORIS WHO?
DORIS STUCK, I CAN'T
MOVE IT AN INCH.

KNOCK, KNOCK.
WHO'S THERE?
DANIELLE.
DANIELLE WHO?
DANIELLE SO LOUD,
WE CAN HEAR YOU
NEXT DOOR!

KNOCK, KNOCK.
WHO'S THERE?
AL.
AL WHO?
AL HUFF AND AL PUFF
AND AL BLOW YOUR
HOUSE DOWN!

KNOCK, KNOCK.
WHO'S THERE?
CATH.
CATH WHO?
OOH, BLESS YOU!

KNOCK, KNOCK.
WHO'S THERE?
MISTER.
MISTER WHO?
MISTER LAST JOKE, DID YOU HEAR IT?

KNOCK, KNOCK.
WHO'S THERE?
ANNIE.
ANNIE WHO?
ANNIE THING WRONG, YOU HAVEN'T BEEN OUT RECENTLY?

KNOCK, KNOCK.
WHO'S THERE?
PICKLE.
PICKLE WHO?
PICKLE-ITTLE BUNCH OF FLOWERS FOR YOUR LOVELY MOTHER.

KNOCK, KNOCK.
WHO'S THERE?
OWL.
OWL WHO?
OWL ABOARD! READY TO SET SAIL!

KNOCK, KNOCK.
WHO'S THERE?
LEE KING.
LEE KING WHO?
LEE KING WATER, AND NOW THERE'S A FLOOD ALL OVER THE ROAD!

145

KNOCK, KNOCK.
WHO'S THERE?
OLIVE.
OLIVE WHO?
OLIVE THE TIMES
I'VE SEEN YOU,
AND YOU STILL
DON'T KNOW ME!

KNOCK, KNOCK.
WHO'S THERE?
RON.
RON WHO?
RON HOUSE, SORRY!
I MEANT TO KNOCK
NEXT DOOR.

KNOCK, KNOCK.
WHO'S THERE?
ALF.
ALF WHO?
ALF OF YOUR ICE CREAM HAS MELTED ON THE DOORSTEP.

KNOCK, KNOCK.
WHO'S THERE?
JOANNA.
JOANNA WHO?
JOANNA PLAY AT THE SKATE PARK?

KNOCK, KNOCK.
WHO'S THERE?
JUANITA.
JUANITA WHO?
JUANITA PIECE OF THIS CAKE THAT I MADE?

KNOCK, KNOCK.
WHO'S THERE?
LAUREN.
LAUREN WHO?
LAUREN ORDER IS VERY MUCH REQUIRED IN THIS TOWN.

KNOCK, KNOCK.
WHO'S THERE?
RUSSELL.
RUSSELL WHO?
RUSSELL ME UP A SANDWICH, I'M STARVING!

KNOCK, KNOCK.
WHO'S THERE?
RILEY.
RILEY WHO?
RILEY, RILEY NEED THE BATHROOM!

KNOCK, KNOCK.
WHO'S THERE?
TRIS.
TRIS WHO?
TRIS IS THE LAST STRAW—JUST LET ME IN!

KNOCK, KNOCK.
WHO'S THERE?
SIDNEY.
SIDNEY WHO?
SID NEEDS YOUR HELP TO FIX HIS CAR.

KNOCK, KNOCK.
WHO'S THERE?
ALF.
ALF WHO?
ALF-OLLOW YOU WHEREVER YOU GO!

KNOCK, KNOCK.
WHO'S THERE?
ALBERT.
ALBERT WHO?
ALBERT YOU CAN'T GUESS WHO IT IS?!

KNOCK, KNOCK.
WHO'S THERE?
TURNER.
TURNER WHO?
TURNER ROUND VERY SLOWLY, THERE'S A ZOMBIE BEHIND YOU!

KNOCK, KNOCK.
WHO'S THERE?
SARA.
SARA WHO?
SARA BETTER TIME FOR ME TO COME OVER?

KNOCK, KNOCK.
WHO'S THERE?
ANNIE.
ANNIE WHO?
ANNIE CHANCE OF
YOU LETTING ME IN?

KNOCK, KNOCK.
WHO'S THERE?
OTIS.
OTIS WHO?
OTIS SUCH A SHAME
YOUR DAD WON'T LET
YOU PLAY!

KNOCK, KNOCK.
WHO'S THERE?
SAVANNAH.
SAVANNAH WHO?
SA, VANNAH VATCH A
MOVIE TOGETHER?

KNOCK, KNOCK.
WHO'S THERE?
PAT.
PAT WHO?
PAT THE TV ON, WE'RE MISSING THE FINAL EPISODE!

KNOCK, KNOCK.
WHO'S THERE?
SHEEP.
SHEEP WHO?
SHEEP-OKES HER NOSE IN EVERYONE'S BUSINESS!

KNOCK, KNOCK.
WHO'S THERE?
DOUBLE.
DOUBLE WHO?
IT'S "W" NOT DOUBLE WHO!

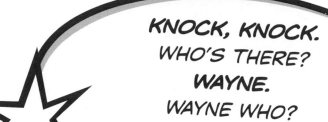

KNOCK, KNOCK.
WHO'S THERE?
WAYNE.
WAYNE WHO?
WAYNE-DEER DON'T JUST APPEAR AT CHRISTMAS, YOU KNOW!

KNOCK, KNOCK.
WHO'S THERE?
EMMETT.
EMMETT WHO?
EMMETT YOU HERE BEFORE! DON'T YOU RECOGNIZE ME?

KNOCK, KNOCK.
WHO'S THERE?
DREW.
DREW WHO?
DREW-PY PANTS ARE AN EMBARRASSMENT!

169

173

KNOCK, KNOCK.
WHO'S THERE?
QUEEN.
QUEEN WHO?
QUEEN WINDOWS MAKE YOUR HOUSE LOOK BETTER!

KNOCK, KNOCK.
WHO'S THERE?
OLGA.
OLGA WHO?
OLGA HOME IF YOU DON'T OPEN THE DOOR!

KNOCK, KNOCK.
WHO'S THERE?
KEN.
KEN WHO?
KEN YOU HELP, I CAN'T CARRY EVERYTHING!

KNOCK, KNOCK.
WHO'S THERE?
MICHAEL.
MICHAEL WHO?
MICHAEL BE OVER LATER WITH HIS NEW GIRLFRIEND.

KNOCK, KNOCK.
WHO'S THERE?
ELIAS.
ELIAS WHO?
ELIAS ALL THE TIME, IT'S HARD TO BELIEVE HIM.

KNOCK, KNOCK.
WHO'S THERE?
IRMA.
IRMA WHO?
IRMA CELEBRITY, GET ME OUTTA HERE!

KNOCK, KNOCK.
WHO'S THERE?
MARSHA.
MARSHA WHO?
MARSHA-MALLOWS IN MY HOT CHOCOLATE, PLEASE!

KNOCK, KNOCK.
WHO'S THERE?
RHODA.
RHODA WHO?
RHODA BIKE FOR THE FIRST TIME TODAY!

KNOCK, KNOCK.
WHO'S THERE?
NEIL.
NEIL WHO?
NEIL-LY FOOLED YOU, IT'S REALLY KEVIN!

187

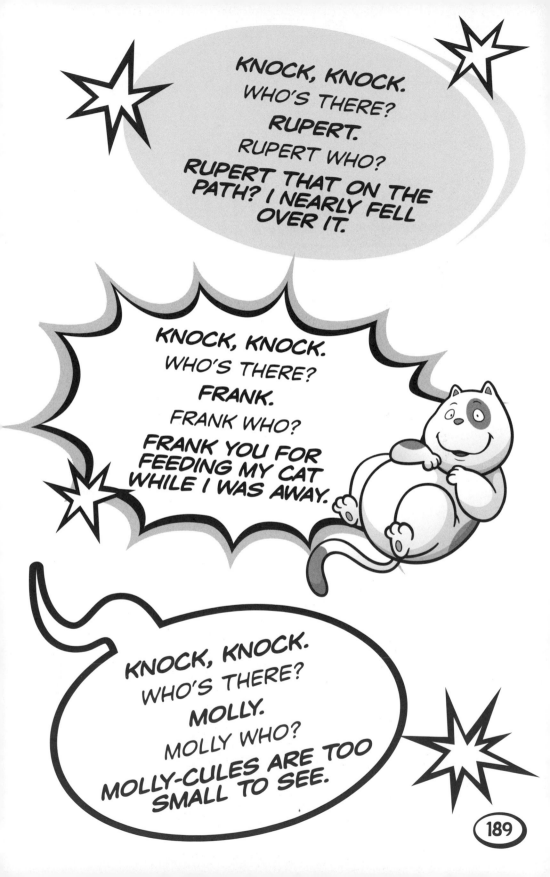

KNOCK, KNOCK.
WHO'S THERE?
STELLA.
STELLA WHO?
STELLA THIS JOKE AND EVERYBODY WILL LAUGH.

KNOCK, KNOCK.
WHO'S THERE?
PAIGE.
PAIGE WHO?
PAIGE YOUR SALARY INTO THE BANK FOR YOU.

KNOCK, KNOCK.
WHO'S THERE?
RICK.
RICK WHO?
RICKETY BRIDGE ON THE WAY HERE, YIKES!

KNOCK, KNOCK.
WHO'S THERE?
OTTO.
OTTO WHO?
OTTOLD YOU TO TURN YOUR MUSIC DOWN!

KNOCK, KNOCK.
WHO'S THERE?
THE INTERRUPTING COW.
THE INTERRUPT C—
MOO!

KNOCK, KNOCK.
WHO'S THERE?
SANDY.
SANDY WHO?
SANDY PIZZA MAN TO MY HOUSE!

193

KNOCK, KNOCK.
WHO'S THERE?
ZAYN.
ZAYN WHO?
ZAYN-EY WAY TO GET YOU TO STOP TELLING JOKES?

KNOCK, KNOCK.
WHO'S THERE?
STORK.
STORK WHO?
STORK ABOUT THE GOOD OLD DAYS.

KNOCK, KNOCK.
WHO'S THERE?
KERRY.
KERRY WHO?
KERRY MY BAGS INTO THE HOUSE, WILL YOU?

KNOCK, KNOCK.
WHO'S THERE?
HANNAH.
HANNAH WHO?
HANNAH-LUJAH,
YOU'RE READY ON
TIME!

KNOCK, KNOCK.
WHO'S THERE?
TEX.
TEX WHO?
TEX ONE TO
KNOW ONE!

KNOCK, KNOCK.
WHO'S THERE?
SODA.
SODA WHO?
SODA BUTTON BACK ON
YOUR SHIRT, DUDE!

200

KNOCK, KNOCK.
WHO'S THERE?
THISTLE.
THISTLE WHO?
THISTLE BE THE FIRST TIME YOU'VE BEEN READY ON TIME!

KNOCK, KNOCK.
WHO'S THERE?
EZRA.
EZRA WHO?
EZRA NO WAY YOU'RE ALLOWED OUT TO PLAY?

KNOCK, KNOCK.
WHO'S THERE?
NOBBY.
NOBBY WHO?
NOBBY AT MY HOUSE SO I WAS LONELY!

KNOCK, KNOCK.
SPARKLE.
SPARKLE WHO?
SPARKLE START A FIRE, WATCH OUT!

KNOCK, KNOCK.
WHO'S THERE?
AMERY.
AMERY WHO?
AMERY CHRISTMAS TO YOU ALL!

KNOCK, KNOCK.
WHO'S THERE?
WEEVIL.
WEEVIL WHO?
WEEVIL, WEEVIL ROCK YOU!

213

KNOCK, KNOCK.
WHO'S THERE?
COSTAS.
COSTAS WHO?
COSTAS A FORTUNE TO GO TO THE RESTAURANT!

KNOCK, KNOCK.
WHO'S THERE?
ASHER.
ASHER WHO?
ASHER NICELY AND SHE'LL MAKE YOU A SANDWICH.

KNOCK, KNOCK.
WHO'S THERE?
ENOCH.
ENOCH WHO?
ENOCH SO MANY TIMES, THEY'VE STOPPED ANSWERING.

217

KNOCK, KNOCK.
WHO'S THERE?
WATER.
WATER WHO?
WATER LOT OF FUSS OVER NOTHING!

KNOCK, KNOCK.
WHO'S THERE?
JUNO.
JUNO WHO?
JUNO WHICH BUS WE NEED TO CATCH?

School Bus

KNOCK, KNOCK.
WHO'S THERE?
ABBY.
ABBY WHO?
ABBY BIRTHDAY TO YOU!

KNOCK, KNOCK.
WHO'S THERE?
NORM.
NORM WHO?
NORM MORE KNOCK KNOCK JOKES, PLEASE!

KNOCK, KNOCK.
WHO'S THERE?
CHUCK.
CHUCK WHO?
CHUCK THE DOOR AGAIN, IT SHOULD BE OPEN.

KNOCK, KNOCK.
WHO'S THERE?
FIFI.
FIFI WHO?
FIFI FO FUM, I SMELL THE BLOOD OF AN ENGLISHMAN!

KNOCK, KNOCK.
WHO'S THERE?
SUNDAY.
SUNDAY WHO?
SUNDAY MY PRINCE WILL COME!

KNOCK, KNOCK.
WHO'S THERE?
CARTER.
CARTER WHO?
CARTER TRYING TO SNEAK OUT WHEN SHE WAS GROUNDED!

KNOCK, KNOCK.
WHO'S THERE?
KENNY.
KENNY WHO?
KENNY COME BACK LATER?

237

KNOCK, KNOCK.
WHO'S THERE?
CLARA.
CLARA WHO?
CLARA SPACE AND I'LL PUT MY BIKE IN THE GARAGE.

KNOCK, KNOCK.
WHO'S THERE?
ICE CREAM SODA.
ICE CREAM SODA WHO?
ICE CREAM SODA PEOPLE CAN HEAR ME!

KNOCK, KNOCK.
WHO'S THERE?
MISCHA.
MISCHA WHO?
MISCHA MORE AND MORE EACH DAY.

KNOCK, KNOCK.
WHO'S THERE?
HOLLY.
HOLLY WHO?
HOLLY UP, WE'LL MISS THE BUS!

KNOCK, KNOCK.
WHO'S THERE?
AHMED.
AHMED WHO?
AHMED A MISTAKE AND I'M REALLY SORRY.

KNOCK, KNOCK.
WHO'S THERE?
FITZ.
FITZ WHO?
FITZ THROUGH MY DOOR, BUT NOT THROUGH YOURS.